GETTING TO KNOW
THE WORLD'S
GREATEST COMPOSERS

J O H A N N E S

BRAHMS

WRITTEN AND ILLUSTRATED BY MIKE VENEZIA

CONSULTANT
DONALD FREUND, PROFESSOR OF COMPOSITION, INDIANA UNIVERSITY SCHOOL OF MUSIC

CHILDREN'S PRESS®
A DIVISION OF GROLIER PUBLISHING
NEW YORK   LONDON   HONG KONG   SYDNEY
DANBURY, CONNECTICUT

To Dagne Strothers
Thanks for the lullabies and for being an inspiration in my life
Love, Mike

Picture Acknowledgements
Photographs ©: Art Resource, NY: 23 (Desterreichische Galerie, Vienna, Austria/Erich Lessing),
6 top (Schubert Museum, Vienna, Austria./Erich Lessing), 4 bottom (Museo Biblioteca Musicale,
Bologna); Corbis-Bettmann: 4 top, 7, 14 left, 18, 30, 32; Mary Evans Picture Library: 3, 6 bottom,
14 right, 15, 17, 31; Yale Center for British Art, Paul Mellon Collection: 5.

Library of Congress Cataloging–in–Publication Data

Venezia, Mike.
    Johannes Brahms / written and illustrated by Mike Venezia.
        p.   cm. — (Getting to know the world's greatest composers)
    Summary: Presents a biography of the nineteenth-century German
composer who combined both classical and Romantic musical styles to
compose his lively songs and powerful symphonies.
    ISBN 0-516-21056-4 (lib. bdg.)   0-516-26467-2 (pbk.)
    1. Brahms, Johannes, 1833-1897—Juvenile literature.
2. Composers—Germany—Biography—Juvenile literature. [1. Brahms,
Johannes, 1833-1897. 2. Composers.]   I. Title. II. Series:
 Venezia, Mike. Getting to know the world's greatest composers.
ML3930.B75V46 1999
780' .92—dc21
[B]
                                    98-30368
                                        CIP
                                  MN AC

Johannes Brahms
as a young man

Johannes Brahms was born in the busy German city of Hamburg in 1833.

He wrote all kinds of music, from lively songs and dances to powerful symphonies. For more than 100 years, kids all over the world have fallen asleep to Brahms's Lullaby, which was originally called "Wiegenlied."

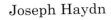
Joseph Haydn

During Johannes Brahms's time, there were two popular but very different styles of music in Germany. One was classical music, which followed certain rules that were never supposed to be broken.

Classical composers, like Joseph Haydn and Wolfgang Amadeus Mozart, created beautiful, well-balanced musical pieces that were perfect for polite gatherings and royal parties. People knew what to expect from classical music and were never surprised by it.

Wolfgang Amadeus Mozart

A European musical gathering in the late 1700s

Franz Schubert

The other style of music was called Romantic. Romantic composers sometimes wrote their pieces to go along with a romantic story or poem. They often added new exciting instrumental sounds to get your attention.

Romantic composers, like Franz Schubert and Felix Mendelssohn, filled their compositions with emotion, personal feelings, and lots of musical surprises.

Felix Mendelssohn

A nineteenth-century cartoon showing an orchestra
playing Romantic music

Johannes Brahms liked some of the ideas
behind both musical styles. In his most
popular pieces, Johannes combined the power
and emotion of Romantic music with delicate,
controlled, classical music.

Johannes Brahms grew up in a very poor family. They lived near Hamburg's waterfront area in a rickety, overcrowded apartment house. Johannes's father was a musician. He knew how to play almost every instrument in the orchestra. When Johannes was only five or six years old, he started to become interested

in music and demanded that his father teach him to play something right away. Johannes was very stubborn and usually got his way.

Mr. Brahms tried to get his son to play an instrument like the violin or cello, which Mr. Brahms knew really well, but Johannes had other ideas.

Johannes wasn't interested in the violin or cello. What he really wanted to play was the piano. Mr. Brahms finally agreed, and began looking for the best teacher he could afford.

Johannes was lucky to have had two excellent piano teachers while he was growing up. When Johannes was very young, a teacher named Wilhelm Cossel worked hard to develop the boy's special talent. Later, a really famous teacher, Eduard Marxsen, took over.

Both teachers were amazed at how quickly Johannes learned to play the piano. They had to get used to working with their student at all hours of the day and night. Johannes loved to practice. He soon became interested in composing music, too.

During his teenage years, Johannes was very busy studying the piano, composing music, and going to school.

In order to help out his family, he also worked late into the night. Johannes made extra money playing dance music in some of the dingiest smoky taverns on Hamburg's waterfront. These were dangerous places filled with strange and creepy customers.

Johannes often brought books along. He read romantic-adventure stories and

poems while he played. Escaping into
stories filled with forests, mountains, and
legendary castles helped keep his mind
off his exhausting job.

Eduard Reményi and
Johannes Brahms

*B*y the time
Johannes was
twenty years old,
he had become an
excellent pianist.
He became friends with a well-known
Hungarian violinist named Eduard
Reményi. Reményi and Brahms decided
to travel around Germany and give
concerts. Johannes learned a lot about
Hungarian and Gypsy folk music from
his friend.

Folk music became an important part
of many of Johannes Brahms's later works.
It gave his music a special fascinating sound.
You can hear exciting Hungarian-Gypsy
melodies in parts of Brahms's Violin Concerto

Gypsies dancing and playing music

in D Minor, in his Piano Quartet No. 1 in
G Minor, and especially in his *21 Hungarian
Dances.*

During his travels, Johannes met some remarkable musicians. One was Franz Liszt, the most famous Romantic-style pianist in the world. Liszt was known to break piano strings with his wild playing. Even though Franz Liszt could have helped Johannes out

A nineteenth-century cartoon showing Franz Liszt at the piano

with his career, Johannes showed little interest in Liszt's music.

Johannes didn't like the group of young musicians who hung around Liszt, either. He thought that they were all a bunch of snobby show-offs, and he couldn't wait to get away from them.

Robert and
Clara
Schumann

Johannes enjoyed the music of Robert Schumann much more. Robert was a famous composer, and his wife Clara was a famous pianist. When Johannes met them at their home, he was asked to play some of his music. Both Robert and Clara couldn't believe their ears! They had never heard such beautiful music.

Robert decided to write an article about Brahms for an important music magazine. He wrote about how amazed he was by the young composer's music and how everyone should keep their eye on Brahms because he was going to be one of the greatest composers ever.

Johannes was surprised by the article. He didn't know if he should be happy or upset. It was nice to be complimented by a famous composer, but Johannes was afraid he might disappoint people.

Thanks to Robert Schumann, when Johannes returned home, he found himself unbelievably famous. He worked as hard as he could to live up to his new reputation. He wrote new piano and violin pieces and performed them at public concerts. Then a terrible thing happened. Robert Schumann became seriously ill.

Johannes traveled to the Schumann's home to see if there was anything he could do. But soon after he arrived, his friend died. Johannes stayed on for a few months helping Clara get over her sadness. He watched her seven children so she could continue to give piano concerts. During this time, Johannes hardly worked on his music. He just didn't have time. People began to worry.

*L*uckily, as soon as Clara was getting along okay, Johannes began composing again. In 1857, he got a job as music director in the court of Detmold. The castle where Johannes taught was in one of the most beautiful forests in all Germany. Johannes loved spending hours hiking through the woods there.

A painting of a German forest by nineteenth-century Romantic
painter Caspar David Friedrich

The giant trees in the forests around
Detmold seemed to give Johannes a certain
energy that inspired all kinds of music.

You can hear Brahms's love of nature in his Second Symphony in D Minor, which he wrote years later. Johannes used lots of oboes, clarinets, and bright, airy flutes that somehow give you a feeling of being outdoors in a wonderful forest with blue skies and bubbling streams.

The Second Symphony was a big hit, which made Johannes very happy. Symphonies are important works, and are very difficult to compose. They are written for a large orchestra and usually have three or four parts that are called movements. Johannes eventually composed four symphonies during his life, but it took him many years before he got up the nerve to try one for the first time.

The reason Johannes felt funny about doing a symphony was because of Ludwig van Beethoven. Beethoven had died a few years before Johannes was born. Many people all over Germany and Europe thought Beethoven was the greatest composer ever. They thought his nine symphonies were as perfect as symphonies could be.

Everyone hoped Johannes might be the next Beethoven and would continue doing the same kind of music. Even though Johannes loved Beethoven's music, he didn't want to be compared to Beethoven. He wanted to be known for his own music.

For much of his life, Johannes Brahms felt like he was living in Beethoven's giant shadow. This feeling bothered him a lot. Even so, in 1876, Johannes finished his First Symphony.

After writing lots of successful concertos, sonatas, songs, and waltzes, Johannes had gotten his confidence up enough to compose a difficult symphony. One of his works in particular had convinced him and his friends that he could do it. It was a piece he wrote in 1868, called *A German Requiem*.

The requiem had a big orchestra and large chorus. It was dedicated to the memory of Johannes's mother, who had just died. Johannes had loved his mother and missed her very much. This was one of Johannes Brahms's most important works. In it, he took the serious subject of dying, and composed music filled with hope and love.

A German Requiem has parts that are sad enough to make some people cry, and parts that have a joyful energy that can make you feel great!

In 1863, Johannes had moved to Vienna, Austria. It was the perfect city for him. Composers like Beethoven, Mozart, and Schubert had lived and died there. Johannes enjoyed the happy lifestyle in Vienna. There were great restaurants, parks, and concerts all over the place. Johannes began to enjoy his success.

A silhouette of Brahms drawn by his friend Otto Bohler

He composed all kinds of music there, including his four symphonies, the famous Violin Concerto, and the fun, exciting *Academic Festival Overture*. He also grew a long beard and went out on lots of dates.

This sketch of Brahms conducting was drawn by his friend Willy von Beckerath.

Johannes Brahms with some young friends

Even though he never got married, Johannes had many close friends. Some of them drew pictures of him or took photographs of him.

Johannes Brahms
at the piano

*J*ohannes Brahms died in 1897. He composed some of the most perfect music ever. Johannes lived long enough to have the honor of being known as one of the "three B's"—Bach, Beethoven, and Brahms.

Brahms's beautiful music can often be heard on classical-music radio stations. Hundreds of CDs and tapes of his music are available at music stores, too.